Remember...

A Love Story

Eve A. Thomas

Cover Images by www.photos.com
Editing by Janet Matthews
Front Cover Design by Mikee Gordon

The names of certain individuals in this book have been changed to protect their identities.

Produced by:

FriesenPress

Suite 300 – 852 Fort Street
Victoria, BC, Canada V8W 1H8

www.friesenpress.com

Distributed to the trade by The Ingram Book Company

TABLE OF CONTENTS

"Author *Eve Thomas* is an ordinary Canadian woman with an extraordinary story: her spiritual connection to the King of Rock and Roll, Elvis Presley.

The reader is quickly transported to Eve's world, where one can't help but ponder: How would I react if the spirit of Elvis Aaron Presley was communicating with me? How would I handle it, knowing that Elvis and I had known each other in another time and place and that our deep love did not die?

Ms. Thomas writes in a comfortable fashion, inviting the reader into her loving relationship with Elvis, while courageously sharing her fascinating and personal story.

The book's details blew me away. I soon forgot the iconic subject, and simply enjoyed and delighted in a love story laced with delicious synchronicity that even the most talented fiction writer could not make up.

Truth is stranger than fiction, and love never dies. Eve's true life story exemplifies this premise."

— Jewelle St. James
Author of *All You Need Is Love - A past life with John Lennon*

ACKNOWLEDGEMENTS

MY SINCERE GRATITUDE to the Kennedy Riddle Production Cast:

Elvis Presley, Carl Sandburg, Sonny Bono, Frank Sinatra, Dean Martin, Sammy Davis, Jr., Peter Lawford, Bing Crosby, Rosemary Clooney, Jackie Kennedy Onassis, John F. Kennedy, Jr., Frank Gorshin and Don Bauer (who does not realize he was part of this production).

Thank you to Elvis Presley and John Baron (Lennon) for connecting me with Jewelle St. James, who has become a very dear friend. Knowing that someone else has experienced past lives with a celebrity and has written about their loving relationship is so comforting.

Thank you Jewelle, for your encouragement and support while I continued through the writing and publishing process. Your endorsement for my work is overwhelming.

Forever Grateful to:

Author Larry Geller, for keeping your promise to Elvis and for writing & publishing the book, *Leaves of Elvis' Garden - The Song of His Soul*. For without this book, I would not have discovered my true identity nor had the courage to write Elvis and my love story.

With Deepest Gratitude to:

Dawne Warner for your loving support and encouragement when I wanted to hide and give up on this project and my dream!

Randy Davila, President of Hampton Roads and Hierophant Publishing for your author workshops and publishing information that helped push me forward to get my manuscript into print.

Family and friends that have supported me on this amazing journey.

For Easa,
Your Eternal and Sacred Love,
Mary

"It's amazing Molly. The love inside, you take it with you."
— Patrick Swayze as character Sam Wheat,
from the movie Ghost (1990)

1
THE BEGINNING

My parents had trouble naming me. Eventually they named me Eva Kathleen but at first they called me Kathy Eva, which even to them did not sound correct! So they named me Eva Kathleen after my father's only sister Eva. Because of this, I always felt like I did not have my own identity and I struggled with that. My family always called me Eve, which seemed to fit better. But eventually I changed my name officially to Eve Alexandra, which I have never regretted; I feel this is who I truly am.

We lived in Bowness, a bedroom community for the City of Calgary and the largest town in Alberta. I had two older sisters and a younger brother, and our childhood was an adventurous and wonderful time. There were hikes, picnics in the hills, hide-and-go-seek, swimming in the river lagoon, playing in our own playhouse, visits to the Shangri-La restaurant to feed the ducks and playing with Sandy the cocker spaniel. I especially loved the summer time, which always seemed like it would go on forever.

Our Grandpa lived right next door to us in a two-room house that still had an outhouse and a well with a pump where he got his water. I don't remember talking to him much, but I was always proud to be seen with him. Sometimes he would go to the river with us, and he would also take us to feed the ducks with breadcrumbs, if we asked. This is one of my fondest childhood memories.

When I was three I started attending Sunday school at a Protestant church. I always felt there was a mission or purpose to my life. I just couldn't seem to figure out what it was. I saw white lights around things and people, but I had no idea why. When I told my sister about it, she didn't seem to know what I meant. Much later I learnt I was seeing the person's energy field, or aura. At the time, no one else I knew ever spoke about this so I never mentioned it again.

There were also times when I just knew things. I remember playing the card game "Pairs," and being able to find the matching card most of the time. Some of this was due to a good memory, but frequently it was because of a kind of "knowing," or intuition. I just knew. I often wondered where I had come from, who was I, and what was I doing here?

When I was about eleven I began experiencing the visions of a woman fully clothed, swimming in deep water, while holding a child. Without question, I knew this woman was me. At the time I thought this must be a vision of some future event, which I found to be quite frightening. I have always been very afraid of deep water. This early childhood vision was one of the reasons I never had any children.

School was difficult as I was a slow reader and never understood what I read. I found most of the information boring, and spent a lot of time reading things over and over until I fell asleep. I mostly felt very lost and lonely. I never felt good about school.

As I got older and progressed through the grades, I continued to struggle. I taught Sunday school, Pioneer Girls and went to the Young Peoples group. I also sang in church with my sisters. This kept me busy, and also provided me with some purpose. I felt God had brought me here for a reason, and it was up to me to figure it out. I still often wondered, "Who am I?"

By the time I was in grade eleven I had started to think that maybe I had been on the earth at another time. Of course at that point I knew nothing about past lives or reincarnation, or how it all might work, but the idea took hold and I could not stop thinking about it. That same year I got a job at F. W. Woolworth's as a waitress in their café. This was hard at first because I was so shy. When I took people's orders, I couldn't look at them; when I delivered their food, I wouldn't know who had ordered what.

There was one gentleman who came into the restaurant regularly; he was a Jehovah's Witness. One time he looked at my name tag, and when he saw my name, he said to me, "Oh, the Mother of All Life." After he left, I couldn't stop thinking about this comment. What if he was right? What if I was the original Eve? How would people treat her if they knew she was back on the Earth? I felt guilty even thinking these thoughts, and didn't want to think that maybe this was my truth. I was sixteen and taking on the sins of the world. No one I knew ever talked about past lives or the idea of reincarnation.

After high school I quit my job at Woolworth's to find fulltime employment as a secretary. I was so shy and had no idea how to present myself in an interview. I lost all my confidence, and the longer I was away from school, the more my secretarial skills diminished.

A friend suggested I take a keypunch course to try and get into that type of work. I thought it was a good idea, so I did. Three months after finishing the course, I finally found a job in the keypunch department of a large oil company. I worked nights five days a week, from 5 p.m. until 10 p.m. It was very busy, but I enjoyed the work. After six months they finally put me on days, and I was very glad to get off of the night shift.

After five years of working with this company I began dating one of the fellows that worked there. I didn't think the fact that he was a Catholic was a problem, but the people at my church thought I was making a mistake. They told me to get back to the "Will of God." This made me very angry.

How do they know what the will of God is, I wondered? He never criticized them for their beliefs, and I thought he was more of a Christian than they were. So I stopped going to church altogether. After dating for a year, we eloped in December of 1977. I was twenty-six years old and very naive.

Unfortunately, my new young husband had health problems and I was constantly worried about not being able to support us if anything should happen to him. We also moved every few years. We would get settled somewhere, and then we would find a reason to move again. I'm not sure if we were running away from something; maybe we were running *to* something.

WHAT DOES 1122 MEAN?

It was in 1986, that I first noticed the numbers eleven twenty-two (1122) and twenty-two eleven (2211) showing up in my life. It happened so often I thought they must be important or significant. I was not sure what to make of this as I had not yet heard of numerology.[1] The first time I saw

---

1 **Numerology** is any study of the purported divine, mystical or other special relationship between a number and some coinciding observed (or perceived) events. Numerology and numerological divination by systems were popular among early mathematicians, such as Pythagoras, but are no longer considered part of mathematics and are regarded as pseudomathematics or pseudoscience by modern scientists. *www.wikipedia.org The Free Encyclopedia*

the number twenty-two eleven was on a very large older home in one of the wealthier areas of our city. The address was 2211 – 7th Street. The couple who first owned and built it had gone to Italy on their honeymoon, and returned home on the Titanic. They both survived the voyage, but their lives were not very happy as he was ostracized by the community because he had survived. The home was now being rented out by its third owners. My husband knew the couple who were renting it, so we were able to visit this home twice during 1986. While I was in the house I felt very strange, and wondered if maybe I had been on the Titanic in a past life.

In 1989, I decided to go to University. I felt I needed that piece of paper to get ahead. I was working for the University at the time. I quit my job to upgrade my high school mathematics and English to meet the requirements, and began classes. Then my husband decided to quit his job, and it was a whole year before he found a new one – this time in British Columbia. So I dropped out of school, we sold our home and moved away from family and friends to start a new life in a new city. I had no job, no university degree, and I felt very discouraged.

A PIECE OF EIGHT

While we were living in Vancouver, the Henry Birks and Sons store brought to Canada some of Mel Fisher's *Nuestra Senora de Atocha* treasures for viewing, and for purchase. In 1622, the *Atocha* had been one of a fleet of twenty-eight Spanish galleon ships, and she had rendezvoused with the vessels of the *Tierra Firme (Mainland) Fleet* in Havana. During the voyage back to Spain, most of the ships sank during a hurricane off the coast of Florida. The *Atocha* had been carrying the largest treasure cargo. Mel Fisher and his family had searched for the *Atocha* and its treasure for sixteen years. In 1985, they finally found a large portion of it.

I was very excited to view this treasure. When I did, there was one piece of jewelry that I just loved. It was a smaller portion of a "piece of eight" – a silver coin surrounded by gold on a gold chain. I really wanted it, but I didn't know why I was so attracted to it. It cost twelve hundred dollars, but with no job I couldn't justify buying it.

I researched information about the "piece of eight" (*peso de ocho*) and found it was a Spanish dollar worth eight reales, about thirty-six millimeters in diameter. The coin I was drawn to was the size of a dime and probably worth one real. I knew I would not be buying it, so I put it out of my mind.

My husband was not happy with his job. After eighteen months, he applied for a contract position back in Alberta and got it. We were on the move again.

Because we had sold everything to move, my sister and her family let us stay with them. My husband really struggled with this. After a couple of months, we found a townhouse to rent and were able to move into our own place. Things seemed to improve somewhat, but we had gone downhill as far as our finances and lifestyle.

Once again, I decided to go back to school. This time I thought I'd try a technical college with a shorter term. A two year program would get me back to work faster, which would really help with our finances. On Orientation Day, as I sat in the front row of the lecture hall, I felt someone staring at me from behind. I glanced around and saw a fellow class-mate staring at me. It gave me the chills, as it felt like looking into the face of someone I'd known from long ago. During our first class he sat right behind me. When I turned around and introduced myself, I saw he was wearing a silver coin surrounded by gold on a gold chain.

"Is that a piece of eight?" I asked, and he replied, "Yes!"

Over the next while I learned that his middle name was Adam. He was very much like me in many of his mannerisms and lifestyle. Was he the original Adam, I wondered? I tried to talk to him about this, but he was clearly not interested in this kind of thing. If someone is not ready for this kind of thinking, there is no point in pursuing it, so we never talked about it again.

During the time we lived in British Columbia, I gained weight, and with going back to school I felt the need to get healthier. I started doing aerobics five times a week, and took swimming lessons once a week. The pounds dropped off and I started to feel very good about myself. I let my hair grow long, and began wearing blue jeans with a blue jean jacket. I didn't realize I was wearing the collar of the jacket standing up. One day, while we were waiting for class, Adam surprised me by commenting, "Eve, you seem to have an Elvis thing going on!" Not knowing how to respond I just laughed it off, as I realized that was how Elvis had worn his jean jacket.

Then I started noticing the numbers twenty-two eleven or eleven twenty-two showing up in my life again. This time it was my semester ID. I was assigned S1122 for my first semester and R2211 for my second semester.

MY SPIRITUAL JOURNEY BEGINS

During my first semester at college my marriage began to seriously fall apart. I asked my husband for a separation. I wanted my own apartment, and he agreed. It was 1993.

I had really put my spiritual side on hold while living with my husband, but I had not forgotten it. Once I was on my own I began reading more books about metaphysical topics. I still had that nagging feeling about past lives – and my identity as Eve. I also started to meditate, and soon discovered I could connect with loved ones and others that had passed over. They frequently gave me messages to pass along to their loved ones. They not only appeared in my meditations, but also in my dreams – and often with profound messages. Whenever this happened, I tried to forward any information I was given to the appropriate people.

After completing college and working as a consultant for a few years, I applied for a job as a technical writer working for a pipeline software company back in Calgary. When I rented a car to drive to the interview, I noticed the license plate number was B11822 and I wondered why there was an eight between the eleven and the twenty-two. I got the job, and found I was excited to be going home.

In the fall of 1998, I bought a townhouse in the south of Calgary not far from my office. The house number was 38, which in numerology equals an eleven. There were fifty-six townhomes in the complex, another eleven. It was located on the east side of Highway 22X. I had not planned any of this, it just happened. I had heard that if numbers appear in multiples (such as 11, 22, 33, 44, etc.), they should not be added together. This seemed to be the case for the eleven and twenty-two that appeared to me.

On November 1st, 1999, I had a telephone reading from Jacquelyne Ellis, an Angel and Spirit Guide Communicator. She had worked with prominent and successful Portland, Oregon, businessman Nick Bunick to help him remember his past life as Paul of Tarsus. During my reading, I asked her about Eve, the numbers eleven twenty-two or twenty-two eleven, and about other information that related to my life. Jacqueline confirmed that I was the original feminine that had come to Earth. The number twenty-two was my Soul master code. The eleven was my human activation number: the number helped activate the memory that I've been here many times, and that people have either not listened to my message, or I felt it was unsafe to speak so I suppressed the truth. She told me I was the Alpha and the Omega, the Beginning and the End. She also confirmed that the story we were originally told about Adam and Eve is false, and that I have the truth within my memory. I found this information overwhelming; I had no idea what to do with it. While the number eight also seemed to be significant, we did not discuss what it might mean. I went on with my daily life, wondering about all I had been told.

I was not yet divorced from my husband. When I asked him to make it official, he found a paralegal to do the paper work and filed it in the summer of 1999. When I received my divorce papers they were dated, November 22, 1999 (11/22/99). We had been married for a total of twenty-two years.

ENTER MARILYN MONROE AND CARL SANDBURG

I soon discovered that one of the other writers at my office had similar spiritual interests, and we frequently got into interesting conversations. One day she told me she had been Marilyn Monroe in her most recent past lifetime. I made no comment; I didn't know whether to believe her or not. Not long after that I had a dream where a very distinguished gentleman appeared. He was dressed in a suit and his hair was parted in the middle. He said nothing and just looked at me. I had no idea who this man might be, or why he had appeared in my dream.

The following Saturday I picked up the August 1999, *People* magazine to read while my hairstylist did my hair. A picture of Marilyn Monroe graced the front cover, and the article was about some of Marilyn's possessions being auctioned off for charity. One of the items was a bust of a man's head – a man whose hair was parted in the middle. Startled, I realized it was the man from my dream. In the article there was a photograph of this man dancing with Marilyn, and the caption identified him as Carl Sandburg, the author. I learned that Carl had been a good friend and father figure to Marilyn.

After the 6:00 o'clock news that evening, there was a show about the auction of Marilyn's things. What am I supposed to figure out here, I wondered? What connection do Marilyn Monroe and Carl Sandburg have to me?

I went to my computer and began searching for information about Carl Sandburg. I learned he was born in 1878 and died on July 22nd, 1967. He was a poet, a writer, and a ballad collector. He wrote about Abraham Lincoln, and had won a Pulitzer Prize for Poetry.

Then I clicked on the link to information about Marilyn Monroe and found a list of the movies she had performed in. The one that caught my eye was *All About Eve* (1950). Had Carl's appearance and this information been to confirm that my friend had indeed been Marilyn and that I had been Eve? I wondered if Carl was going to somehow help me write my story.

MY FIRST PAST LIFE REGRESSION

I went for my first past life regression soon after that. Before we began I asked the woman to take me to the lifetime that was affecting me the most in this lifetime. At first, I saw nothing but darkness. Then she asked me to look at myself, and asked about my body. When I did, all I saw were wisps – like filaments of a cloud. I also saw a group of beings all illuminated with golden light. There was one that stood out in front and was waving at me as I went by. I felt like I was leaving on a journey. This little one reminded me of the cartoon character, *Casper the Friendly Ghost*, except that he was in normal human proportion. During the rest of the regression experience I went into a life I thought must have been that of Adam and Eve. I was not wearing any clothes. I saw someone I thought must be Adam from behind, but I did not see his face. He was working with plants in the ground in a place where there were lots of trees, and a pretty stream.

Unfortunately, the room I was in was very cold; even though I was covered with a blanket I had become uncomfortable and wanted to end the experience. Sadly, I did not feel I had had a very successful regression session.

LEARNING TO MEDITATE SAFELY

After this regression, I started to meditate more. But I knew nothing about protecting myself, and soon found a lower entity living around me. A co-worker had brought an Angel board into my home, thinking it was safe to use. The Angel board turned out to be very similar to a Ouija board. I didn't understand that a person could connect to all manner of entities (spirits) through the board, which may not be Angels. When I finally realized what had happened I stopped meditating and quickly put the board away and out of the house. After doing some research on how to protect myself from lower entities, I put rock salt around my bed for protection and started carrying a rose quartz crystal. Another friend said this spirit was a priest from the 1600s, and that I should keep busy to make him feel unwelcome. He said this priest was very lazy and just wanted to lie around, but with my busyness he would move along. This plan of approach worked and he left, but I was not ready to start meditating again. This had not been a pleasant experience and I did not want to repeat it.

I did not start to meditate again until 2003, when I found Dr. Wayne Dyer's book, *Getting in the Gap*. This book teaches you to mediate using the first ten words of the Lord's Prayer. This felt very good to me, and I felt safe to begin meditating again.

JESUS APPEARS

In 2005, Jesus started to appear during my meditation. It really felt as if we knew each other. Quite often we would be walking on a beach holding hands, or He would have His arm around me. Once I saw a golden necklace lying in the sand, and He picked it up and gave it to me. It was a gold chain with some kind of medallion or coin hanging from it. Could this be the reason I had been so attracted to the necklace from the *Atocha*? Had Jesus given me a similar necklace, long ago? I did not know why I had these visions of being with Jesus. Were they memories of a past life? It felt so good to be in His presence! I also thought about my classmate Adam, and wondered how he fit into this story, especially since it was he who had the necklace with the coin on it.

2
ELVIS APPEARS

On June 5th, 2006, Elvis Presley walked into my meditation wearing his black leathers from the '68 *Comeback Special*, ELVIS. He was singing *All Shook Up*, and appeared as he had at age thirty-three. He then told me that soon I would have other famous people appearing to me.

I had heard on the radio that it was some kind of an anniversary, but I had not paid much attention to the announcer. A quick internet search revealed it to be the 50th Anniversary weekend celebration of Elvis returning to his hometown of Tupelo, Mississippi, as a rock star. I was not, and had never been, an Elvis fan, so I had no idea why he might have shown up in my meditation. I didn't own any of his music or videos, and when we were kids Mom had never allowed us to see any of his movies.

My family had watched Charles Dickens' *A Christmas Carol* every Christmas. I now wondered if I might be living the role of Scrooge when he had three spirits visit him on

Christmas Eve! I wasn't sure I wanted more famous people to appear in my meditations.

I continued to meditate, and then on June 11th, 2006, no fewer than ten famous people appeared. It was a bit mind-boggling. When they appeared, they were arranged as if waiting for a group photograph, in three rows. The first one I noticed was Sonny Bono, and I heard one of his songs, *Baby Don't Go*, which he and Cher recorded and made famous in 1964. Then I noticed, one after the other, Frank Sinatra, Dean Martin, Sammy Davis, Jr., Peter Lawford, Bing Crosby, Rosemary Clooney, Jackie Kennedy Onassis, and John F. Kennedy, Jr. They were arranged like this:

Sonny Bono, Frank Sinatra, Dean Martin, Sammy Davis, Jr.
Rosemary Clooney, Bing Crosby, Peter Lawford
Jackie Kennedy, John F. Kennedy, Jr.

Then, looking right at me Rosemary Clooney said, "George needs you."

What could she mean, I wondered? Did she mean George Clooney? Why would George Clooney need me? I thought to myself, Yeah right!

Then Jackie Kennedy spoke to me. She was holding a picture of President John F. Kennedy and, looking right at me, she said, "He has reincarnated."

There was one man out in front of them all – but just his face. I recognized him as an impressionist named Frank something, from seeing him on the *Ed Sullivan Show*. I had not cared much for his performances because he made such ugly contortions with his face during his impressions. I could not recall his last name, but I thought, Oh no, not this star!

Here were all these famous dead people looking at me, and I was truly overwhelmed, to say the least. Was all of this real or true in any way? I didn't know what to think, so I asked for a sign – something to help validate all these people coming through. I really thought I should know Frank's full name.

When I ended my meditation, I was a bit stunned by what had just happened. I went downstairs and turned on the television to *Turner Classic Movies*. There was a movie already playing, but I didn't know what it was called. As I sat there watching the next scene, in walked the impressionist – Frank! I was amazed at how quickly I received my sign. The *TV Times* revealed it to be the movie *Where the Boys Are*, with Connie Francis. I had not realized Frank was in that movie, and when he appeared I was totally shocked. I now felt this whole experience must be very important. I mean, why else would all of these people appear to me?

A quick internet search brought up the cast list for *Where the Boys Are*. Frank was listed, his last name now revealed as Gorshin. Further searching also revealed the movies and TV shows in which he had appeared, and I quickly discovered he had played *The Riddler* in the original *Batman* television series. The mention of *Batman* also connected me back to George Clooney. They must have known I like a good mystery and would not give up until I figured it out. With Frank being the Riddler, I realized this had definitely become a riddle!

To my surprise, as I scanned the list of movies I noticed that Frank Gorshin had appeared in *All Shook Up* (1999). This connected me back to Elvis singing when he first appeared. I knew nothing about this movie until this moment. When I clicked on the link that took me to the movie's website, I learned the movie was all about Elvis still being alive. On the website, the producer, Don Bauer listed a number of unusual incidents that had occurred during filming. These included microphones that moved across the set that they could not control, cast members who had seen a man dressed in black standing in the distance, and a motor home that just "showed up" for the cast to use for wardrobe changes. There had been no money in the budget for this type of vehicle, and no one had any idea who had sent it. The film had not been released, and they were being sued for breach of contract.

When I read about the unusual events that had occurred during filming I decided to write to Don Bauer about Frank Gorshin. I sent an email that day and explained the information from my meditation about Elvis and Frank. I did not mention the rest of the famous people, as I was not sure if I would hear from him.

The next morning I was surprised to receive an email from Don with a thank you. He said he had enjoyed working with Frank, who had passed away the year before from lung cancer.

In the evening of June 12th I was meditating again, and Sammy Davis, Jr. appeared to me – this time alone. He was sitting in an armchair, and wore a three piece suit with a pocket watch and fob in the vest pockets. He just sat there by himself. He did not say anything, but just looked at me. I thought maybe he had appeared by himself because so many famous people appearing all together had overwhelmed me the previous day.

I ended the meditation and I tried to figure out what the connection was between all these people. My spirit guides told me it was the year 1964, so I looked up information on the internet about the original Rat Pack, and the year 1964. I learned the song *Baby Don't Go* was recorded in 1964, by Sonny and Cher. Frank Sinatra, Dean Martin, Sammy Davis, Jr., Peter Lawford, and later Bing Crosby were all part of the 1960s Rat Pack. I looked for any information that had to do with these people and the year 1964.

I learned that Frank Gorshin had made his first appearance on the *Ed Sullivan Show* in 1964, on the same night the Beatles first appeared.

There were a lot of Elvis connections to 1964. He filmed *Viva Las Vegas* and *Roustabout* that year. He owned a guitar, a 1964 Gretsch Chet Atkins Country Gentleman.

The fact that Rosemary Clooney was one of the people in my meditation made me think this might have something to do with George Clooney and *Batman*. Rosemary was George's Aunt. Then there was her message to me, "George needs you." George had also played Batman in the movie, *Batman & Robin*, and starred in *Ocean's 11*, which was filmed with the original Rat Pack in 1960. George had recently acquired the rights to *Robin and the Seven Hoods*, and I learned the original *Robin and the Seven Hoods* was filmed in 1964. During my research, I also saw the Clooney family referred to as "the Kennedys of the South."

Because Don Bauer had replied so quickly, I thought he might be able to help me understand the rest of this riddle. I emailed him again with the rest of the story to see if he had any insights. He did not reply, and his website was eventually removed.

Over the next two years I tried to figure out what the connection was between all these people, and what to do about it. Because the first person I'd noticed was Sonny Bono and the entire experience was accompanied by his song, *Baby Don't Go*, I knew the year 1964 had to be the common element connecting them all.

Because of Jackie's words to me, "He has reincarnated," as she held the photo of JFK, I strongly felt that the message or riddle was to figure out who JFK was now. Rosemary's words, "George needs you," suggested that it might be someone who was close to George Clooney, and who was born in 1964. Because of all these clues I now believed that 1964 was when

Kennedy had reincarnated, and I needed to discover who he was now.

At first I thought it might be George Clooney, but I ruled him out when I learned he was born in 1961. Then I thought maybe it might be George's good friend Rande Gerber, who is Cindi Crawford's husband, but I was unable to confirm Rande's birthday. A few months had passed now, and at that point, I gave up looking and just hoped to someday figure it out. Every so often I'd look things up on the internet, but I was working full time and running errands for an aging parent. My life was very full at the time, and solving this riddle was just not my highest priority.

I continued to meditate, and then I started doing automatic writing. My first attempt at automatic writing had been back in the 1990s. Someone by the name of Gladys had come through and drawn a flower. I don't know any Gladys, I thought, so I stopped trying to connect to the other side in this way. I eventually realized the Gladys I had connected with had been Elvis' mother and was sorry I had not continued.

ABRAHAM

It was now January 2007, and I heard about Esther and Jerry Hicks. I discovered that Abraham was a group of beings that communicate through Esther Hicks, so I started reading one of their books about the Law of Attraction. This was very fascinating. I felt frustrated that I was not moving forward with my spiritual development more quickly. There must be someone who could appear to help me with my spiritual growth, I thought.

I also listened to some of Abraham's audio recordings. As I listened to the information about intentions, I learned that I should focus on what I wanted for my life and not on how I was going to get it; I should intend that it was already on its way! I learned to focus on things I loved, and that emotions were very important in manifesting your dreams.

I was meditating when I first felt the presence of Abraham. I remembered from the audio recordings that they had moved Esther's head to form the letters of the alphabet, which they also did with me. Then, I decided to try once again to communicate through automatic writing. I picked up a pen and placed my hand on a note pad. I was surprised that the pen started to move. The movements were slow at first. It almost looked like my printing from when I was first learning to write. I was very surprised that they would choose to communicate with me in this way, especially since they communicate through Esther.

On January 16th, they told me they had come to teach me the laws of the universe. They told me there were many with me and they were glad I was open to learning. They said it was important for me to trust and to "keep the FAITH," so to speak. There was so much happening around me and it was important for me not to give up.

I was thinking about taking a cruise with my family and they encouraged me to go. Their message was, "This cruise is part of the plan and going with your family is important as there are things that will occur on this trip that will aid in your growth and power. We need you to go and have a good time. ENJOY! Take a break! We love you, ABRAHAM."

On January 27th, 2007 Abraham wrote the following message to me:

> A long time ago, far away, there lived a wonderful girl. She had many gifts and she was special to all those she knew. This was a wonderful life and she was very happy living there. She was told that there was a place out in space that had lots of boys and girls, but

they didn't laugh and play like she did. They were hungry and lonely. Many of them had no homes. They lived in very bad conditions. They lived without Hope.

One day, a very wise One came to her and asked if she would journey to such a place to help the children to once again laugh and smile? She thought about this question for a while. It would mean leaving those she loved and journeying far away. It meant she would not see home for a while and would go to harsher conditions for the sake of the children. She was happy, but saw the great need on this other world.

The wise One said that she would never be alone, and that if she believed, all her gifts and knowledge would go with her. There were also others that would go to this place as well. They would be in other parts of the world, but one day they would be united as they had work to do together.

This is that time! Soon you will be united with those that have come to this world for One purpose! To heal the World!

Some know that they have a mission. Others are still searching. You will be given more knowledge as time goes by. We are happy that you've come, as this is your destiny!

All of this time you have been preparing,
ABRAHAM

Was this my truth or just a nice story?

3
TITANIC REMEMBERED

On April 1st, 2007, I flew to San Diego to board a ten-day Mexican Riviera Cruise with my brother and his family. I had only cruised once before, back in 2001, and I had really enjoyed the experience. The thought of traveling to new places by ship was thrilling.

I had not paid any attention to the dates of the cruise, which were April 2nd - April 12th, as I'm not a superstitious person. I have always felt I am protected. During the first afternoon aboard ship, they held a lifeboat drill. On my first cruise, we'd been late boarding and missed this procedure, so I didn't know that lifeboat drills are held on all cruise ships. After all the passengers were gathered on deck at our assigned lifeboat stations, we were given the instruction, "Women and children up front." There I stood up front, with my lifejacket on, completely by myself. For some reason I began thinking about all those people on the Titanic, and I became very emotional. When we left the dock in San Diego

I also felt quite sad and a bit homesick. What was the matter with me, I wondered, and why am I so upset?

Our first evening at sea was casual, but the second evening was a formal affair. For the formal evening, I dressed in a long gown and decided to have my photograph taken by the ship's photographer. It never occurred to me that there might be an image on the background screen, and I did not look. They told us the pictures would be posted at the photographer's studio the next day, if we wished to purchase one. When I arrived the next day to see my picture, the sign above the board where they were posted read: *Titanic Photos.* I was startled to discover the background of the photograph was the elegant Grand Staircase from the Titanic! Again I wondered – had I been on the Titanic?

Our trip down the Pacific coast was lovely. This experience was entirely new to me, and I thoroughly enjoyed seeing each of the ports. Cabo San Lucas was the last port on our return voyage, and I especially loved my time there. I was sad to leave as this marked the end of a great holiday. There were two other cruise ships in port and, as we got underway to depart, the other ships blew their horns. The passengers on the other ships' decks began to wave and shout goodbye. Without warning, I started to cry. I could not understand why I was having such a problem with my emotions. Again, I felt it must have something to do with the Titanic. I thought back to being, at the home of that couple who had survived the sinking of the great ship. This was all really starting to feel like déjà vu.

April 11th, 2007 was our last day at sea. Suddenly, while we were finishing our dessert after dinner, the ship started to vibrate and shake. The lights went out and everyone gasped! Then the emergency lights came on, and after a while, the captain came on the speaker and explained that there were electrical problems with the engines. He said we could not go as fast as they wanted, and this would result in a late arrival into San Diego. Once again I was reminded of the Titanic, as the captain of that ship had her going very fast when they hit the iceberg. Our ship was also going fast. The ocean was rough and we were hitting the waves quite hard.

After dinner, as we headed down a staircase to our state-rooms, the lights went out again. It was pitch black and we could not see anything. Luckily there was a gentleman at the bottom of the staircase with a flashlight, and he told us to stand still until he shone his light onto the stairs ahead of us. When we reached our deck, there were no lights on in the hallway, or in the washroom in my room. There were soon more problems with the ship, and eventually they had to shut down the engines altogether. The cruise line then flew a special maintenance person out from the mainland to diagnose and repair the problems.

It was amazing, really, that we were only two hours late arriving in San Diego. But it was enough to make us miss our flight, and we had to call our travel agent and ask her to re-schedule us. We arrived home on Friday, April 13th, 2007, at 12:30 a.m. It was during the evening of April 14th, 1912 that the Titanic hit the iceberg. She sank early in the morning of April 15th.

On April 13th, Abraham wrote to welcome me home, and let me know they knew some of my trip was not that enjoyable. They told me the purpose had been to help me develop more confidence in travelling to other places. When I asked about the Titanic, they confirmed that, yes, there had been Souls on board our ship that had been on the Titanic. Apparently this is why I was feeling so emotional about those who died in the sinking. The electrical problems we experienced were to get my attention. Souls on the other side can manipulate electricity more easily than other things, to let people know they are there. During this experience, the Souls from the Titanic were trying to communicate with me. They wanted me to know they were there, and that I was not alone.

On April 16th Abraham finally confirmed that indeed, I had been on the Titanic. The experience of this trip was in remembrance of that voyage. These were memories of a past life that were surfacing, and they told me it was to help me remember even further back. I had more than once expressed a desire to remember my past lives, and to know my purpose in this lifetime. They told me there was still more for me to remember.

After our trip, I met a friend for coffee and started to tell her about our adventure. When I told her about the engine problems, I said it really was, "A night to remember." My friend started to laugh; she told me that was the title of a movie made years ago about the Titanic. I didn't know about this 1958 docudrama of the Titanic story until I looked it up in my *Movies on TV* book.

For future reference, I had documented the events of our trip in my journal. On April 22nd, Abraham thanked me for recording this information. They then told me this story would be part of the book I would write titled, *Remember*. They said they were excited for me to start writing about my life and memories. They told me they would help me formulate my thoughts, and help me remember.

At this point, I did not think my story would be of interest to anyone.

4
FINDING LARRY AND JESSE

Jesus had been with me now since 2005, and Elvis had been with me since 2006. I still had not solved the "Kennedy Riddle," and I was not sure what my future would hold.

Abraham continued to write until June 12th, 2007, when they introduced me to my new spirit guides, a group of Spirit beings by the name of Olasck. They told me they had come to answer my questions about my new life. They also wanted to help me with my vibrational rate, and my continued spiritual growth. They did help me raise my vibration and, as a result, on August 8th, 2007, Elvis started to connect to me more frequently and more clearly.

TWIN SOULS

On August 26th, Elvis first told me that I was his Twin Soul, and this was why he had been appearing to me over the past year-and-a-half. He said we should have been together in his last lifetime. He told me he missed me so much, and it felt like a part of him was missing. He told me he was sending me love. I think I went into a kind of shock, because I had no idea whether to believe this or not. There were many times that I doubted that the message was actually coming from Elvis. But he patiently continued to remind me that this was true. It was all very amazing. I felt such love coming from him.

Elvis continued to appear in my meditations, and connect to me. He encouraged me to keep going with my spiritual path, and to focus on peace and love. As I continued to meditate Elvis would usually appear and, if he did not, Jesus would appear. I felt the same love and familiarity with both of these Spirit beings.

On January 8th, 2008, I wished Elvis a Happy Birthday. He thanked me for my kind thoughts and recognition; he also told me it was not yet time to tell others of my experiences and our connection. For almost two years I had been silent about my inner experiences, reluctant to share them with anyone.

Then Elvis told me that in 1935, I had come into this world with him as Jesse, his stillborn identical twin brother. He also told me I was his Twin Flame, and that our story was, "A Love Story." I did not know what to think. Could this be true, I wondered? He had told me in August of 2007 that I was his Twin Soul. Were the concepts of Twin Flame and Twin Soul the same? I needed more information. Not having been a fan, I knew very little about Elvis' life, so I started to do more research about him, along with the concepts of Twin Flames and Twin Souls.

GETTING TO KNOW ELVIS

Elvis knew I needed more information about his life and what he believed, so he directed me to the website of his longtime friend, hairstylist, and spiritual mentor, Larry

Geller. I had not heard of Larry before and, I was intrigued to learn that Elvis had been a very spiritual man.

Back in 1957, when Larry was still in high school, Elvis had performed at the Pan-Pacific Auditorium close to where Larry lived. With no tickets, Larry and his buddies thought maybe they could sneak in through a side door of the auditorium. As they came around the side of the building they saw Elvis talking with some of his bodyguards. Larry called to his friends to go with him, but on that evening, he was the only one that got to meet Elvis and shake hands with the King of Rock 'n' Roll.

Larry, of course, had no idea they would one day meet again, and eventually work together. The first movie set they worked on together was *Roustabout* in 1964. After that their friendship grew and Larry worked with Elvis until the day he died in August of 1977, when Larry did his hair for the last time at the funeral home.

Before his sudden death, Elvis had made Larry promise to write the truth about his life and spiritual beliefs. He really wanted the world to know the real Elvis. After many years Larry's book, which is called *Leaves of Elvis' Garden - The Song of His Soul*, had finally been published and Elvis told me to order a copy.

I could hardly wait for it to arrive. Larry's website said there were a few autographed copies available. When mine came I was surprised to discover it was one of those. Elvis told me this was his gift to me, even though Larry said in the book that Elvis had wanted it to be written for Lisa Marie.

Until I read Larry's book, I didn't really know Elvis, but I quickly learned that many of my own spiritual beliefs and life experiences were similar to his. The thing that affected me the most was reading that when he was born, the house had been illuminated in Blue light. This reminded me of the Star that shone down on the place where Jesus was born.

Were they the same person, I wondered? Was this why Elvis sang so much about blue? If I was his twin soul, would this explain why I was so fascinated with the word, "blue?" In the book, Larry also said that Elvis was a healer and had used blue light to heal people, including his own father. He also said Elvis' number was an eight. The more I read, the more curious I became.

Apparently, Elvis had been fascinated by numbers, letters and words, so Larry had provided him with a growing library of mystical and exotic books. Elvis was particularly interested in numbers, so Larry brought him every book on numerology he could find. This was especially intriguing to me, as numbers had played such an important part in my past. Then Elvis discovered that the letters in the Hebrew alphabet were all assigned numbers. He wondered about his own name, and when he looked into it discovered that "Elvis" in Hebrew equaled the number eight. When I used the numeric values of the letters for my own name from the Hebrew alphabet, I discovered it also equaled an eight. Had I just stumbled onto a form of proof that I really was Jesse? Was this the reason the number eight kept showing up in my life, alongside or in between the numbers eleven and twenty-two? From this point on, numbers became even more important to me, and I began watching carefully for more synchronicities regarding the influence of numbers on my life.

Elvis had said not to tell people about my experiences with him. That was no problem – I really didn't want people to think I was an Elvis fanatic. I didn't tell anyone that I wondered if Jesus and Elvis might be the same person, either. Sometimes, you just have to go with your inner truth.

ANGELIC HEALING

I realized if I was going to learn more about spirituality, I needed to involve myself in some type of formal study, and a healing/energy course seemed a good way to start. I thought first about Reiki (because I was familiar with it), and found a local instructor. When I contacted her, she told me she was not teaching beginner Reiki classes any longer, but would I be interested in learning Angelic Healing?

Intrigued, I decided to take this workshop. It was to be held in April of 2008 on two consecutive weekends. I had never done anything like this before, but felt I was being guided, as both Jesus and Elvis had been healers.

5
ELVIS' SURPRISE

Moving forward with my spiritual path was not an easy choice, as I didn't know anyone else doing energy healing work. I had told very few people about my inner experiences with Elvis over the past two years. I was still unsure if Elvis and Jesus might be the same person, so I usually left out my inner connection to Jesus in conversation. People seemed more fascinated by my connection to Elvis than Jesus anyway, and after all, I figured, who was I to be so familiar with the Son of Man? Elvis and Jesus looked nothing alike to me, as Jesus always appeared with the face of a picture I had in my Bible, and Elvis – looked like Elvis.

I registered in the Angelic Healing workshop scheduled for April 5th and 6th, 2008. During the first morning session we began learning about energy healing, and how to use psychometry to receive information and messages from someone else's personal item. We also did a guided meditation. We were told that during the afternoon session we would begin to practice using healing energy on each other.

At the break, four of us decided to go out for lunch together. As soon as we sat down in the restaurant, the other three looked at me, clearly startled, and said, "Eve, you're blue!" Concerned, they wondered if they should take me to emergency! But I felt fine, and simply knew it was Elvis that had turned me blue. I realized Elvis now wanted me to tell the others he was there, but I was still afraid. I had no idea what their reaction might be, so I told them it was a message for me, and left it at that. I never even thought to check the colour of my hands. He had never done anything like this to me before, and I was very surprised he'd taken matters into his own hands in this way. At the end of the lunch one woman said, "So Eve, are you going to tell us?"

"Am I still blue?" I asked.

"Only your nose," she responded with a chuckle.

Considering what had just happened, I decided I would tell them a bit about my Elvis connection. When we got back to class I told them of my experiences with Elvis, and about the Kennedy riddle. I wanted the instructor to hear my story as well, as she had not gone to lunch with the rest of us. I also mentioned the numbers eleven twenty-two and twenty-two eleven. One of the women reminded me that President Kennedy was killed on November 22nd, 1963.

We began another session of meditations, and Elvis appeared in mine wearing a royal blue velvet shirt. Then we started the healing sessions. To help these women with their healing sessions, I envisioned the same colour of blue as Elvis was wearing surrounding each of them. The instructor was guided to have me work on the first woman using the healing techniques we were learning. I knew that Elvis was there guiding me. This turned out to be a very profound and awe inspiring weekend.

On April 11th, 2008, just a few days before the next weekend workshop, I had a dream where I saw a pillow with many wedding bands on it, and I felt I was supposed to pick one. I heard the words, "The Bridegroom Cometh," which is a quote from the Bible regarding the time when the Son of Man will return to claim his Bride. I also heard Elvis singing the words, "Lay Your Head Upon My Pillow," followed by the song, *It's Impossible.*

What was the meaning of this dream? I felt it must indicate something significant for my future – or maybe it was about my past? Did this mean I would be getting married – or had been married – to Jesus?

A STARTLING PAST LIFE REGRESSION

On the second weekend for Angelic Healing II, two more people joined the class. We would be learning how to see auras, give Angel Card readings, and after lunch we would work on past life regressions. Everyone was excited to see what would happen next. I was nervous, as I had no idea what to expect. I had never turned blue before, and realized that Elvis has a great sense of humour!

Prior to this, I had tried past life regressions with little success. Today we first did a meditation to help open the third eye. After lunch, the group looked at me and told me my forehead was red around the area of my third eye! No one else had their third eye turn red, just me. Then we did two regressions.

During my first regression, I found myself standing on a dirt road. I was a man wearing a knee-length white tunic, with gold trim around the lower edge and over the shoulder. I had blondish hair, and wore a gold crown on my head and sandals on my feet. I seemed to be royalty. I saw trees in the distance, and there was no one else on the road.

When I started to tell the others in the workshop what I was wearing and where I was standing, one of them blurted out, "You have a crown on your head." I had intended to leave that bit out of my description, but she said it before I could say anything else. Apparently she could see what I was seeing. That was a shock, as I had never before experienced someone being able to view my thoughts. I was also self-conscious about appearing to be boastful, especially after telling them about Elvis.

In my second regression, I was a young man from Bombay, India. I was an elephant trainer, about twenty-five years old. The elephants were working animals, and mostly hauled logs. I could communicate with them, and I loved them very much. At the end of this lifetime, I died alone; only the elephants remained.

Then we moved along to another lifetime. I heard and saw the name "Moses." I was Moses? I saw the princess looking at the basket in the Nile, then I quickly advanced and saw myself as an older Moses, standing in front of Pharaoh. I threw down my rod and watched it turn into a serpent. The man standing next to me was my brother, Aaron. Aaron was Elvis. I then saw different scenes from this lifetime, but the most important to me was Elvis. I realized that the first regression of me as the man in the white tunic with the crown was also of Moses. I was dressed as royalty, and this would have been when I was younger and lived with the Pharaoh.

This last regression was a significant lifetime from the Bible, and it was a lifetime with Elvis. I remembered that Larry had written about Elvis' mother telling Elvis that his middle name, Aaron, was special and that it connected him to Moses, as Aaron was Moses' brother. I was not sure if the information was true, nor if I wanted to share this with anyone. Before doing that, I would need to learn more about this lifetime, if possible.

Elvis did not turn me blue during this workshop, but my forehead had turned red. What would Elvis do next, I wondered?

TWIN FLAMES EXPLAINED

On April 16th, Elvis directed me to Elizabeth Claire Prophet's website. She had written a book about Twin Flames. On this website I found the answers to my questions about what it meant to be a Twin Flame.

Not everyone's Twin Flame may be available in this life, or is your same age, she explained. They may or may not be a part of your life's purpose. Your Twin Flame could be a baby or even still be waiting to be born into the world, or perhaps even be an Ascended Master.

I learned that your purpose in this lifetime may not be to meet with your Twin Flame, but that all you do positively in your lifetime helps your Twin Flame. So your life's service, love and all your energy is also available to your Twin Flame. This will help balance karma, so you can once again be reunited. After reading this information I finally knew that I had been Elvis' stillborn identical twin brother Jesse, and that I am his Twin Flame.

6
ALASKAN CRUISE

In July of 2008, I went on an Alaskan cruise with some family members. I'd never been to Alaska, but all the others had experienced this wonderful place. I did not know if Elvis had any plans with me for this trip. After meeting my family in Vancouver, we boarded the ship and began our cruise up the coast.

The first port was Juneau, Alaska. I wanted to go shopping for some souvenirs, and the Port & Shopping Ambassador had provided us with information on the best places to shop. He also mentioned they sold blue, pink, yellow, and white diamonds in Juneau. I had never heard of blue diamonds, and had a strong feeling that Elvis wanted me to go look at rings for myself. This is not something I would normally do, but I felt I should at least go and look.

I went to one of the recommended Jewelers and started looking at the rings. A very nice sales woman offered her help. I chose a ring to try on with a setting called Past, Present and Future. It held a blue diamond in the centre of a row of three diamonds. The woman was new, so the store manager came out to help. I tried on a few other rings, but ultimately decided on the first one, planning to wear it on my right hand.

The manager also brought out a tanzanite ring with an antique setting for me to try on my left hand. Tanzanite is a purple gemstone, and this one was in the shape of a triangle. He told me to wear it with the point facing down to make my finger look longer. I inwardly got the message from Elvis that it represented the *Divine Feminine*.

The manager also showed me a matching pendant, but the point of the triangle was facing upwards, while the point in the ring stone was facing down. To me these triangles represented male and female. It also reminded me of the Star of David. I knew I needed to purchase both rings and the pendant. I had never bought anything so extravagant for myself before.

We had a wonderful Alaskan holiday. When I got home, I realized I needed to wear the diamond ring on my left ring finger, as it was too tight for my right hand. I also felt that Elvis wanted me to wear them opposite to how I was wearing them. I knew he had guided the sales staff in the selection of the jewelry I purchased. I had no idea then how important and significant this was for my future with him.

7
KENNEDY RIDDLE SOLVED

By August of 2008, I had still not solved the riddle of who President Kennedy is now. Over the years I had continued trying to figure out what the connection was to all of these famous people, and what to do about it.

I was still looking to confirm Rande Gerber's birth date, with no luck. Then, when I told a friend my story, she did a search and within half an hour was able to confirm that Rande was not born in 1964. I thought it was amazing that she had found his birth date so quickly, and felt it must be Divine Timing! With that question solved, I began my search again. I was again searching for someone who was close to George Clooney and whose birthday was in 1964.

I now began to analyze the people who had shown up in my meditation. Sammy and Frank Gorshin were the most predominant, and both were impressionists. The last person to appear was Sammy Davis, Jr. After examining all the information again, I realized that Sammy had appeared by himself sitting in the armchair in a three-piece suit, reminding me of the statue of President Lincoln. For me, this reference to "The President" was confirmation that President Kennedy had reincarnated as an African American. This also connected me back to Carl Sandburg's book about Abraham Lincoln that I'd discovered in 1999. I had not realized that Carl Sandburg's appearance, and all the information about Marilyn Monroe all those years earlier, was a pre-cursor to this amazing riddle!

Now I could narrow my search to an African American male that was close to George Clooney, and born in 1964. When I researched men who met those qualifiers, I discovered that Don Cheadle was born on November 29th, 1964 (11/29/1964). President Kennedy was killed on November 22nd, 1963 (11/22/1963), and Don was born a year later.

I then started researching information about Don Cheadle. What did he do, and what films had he completed? Then I discovered he had actually portrayed or impersonated Sammy Davis, Jr. in the 1998 Rat Pack movie! This was the missing piece that confirmed to me that Don was the solution to the riddle. Plus, the appearance of the original Rat Pack in my meditation also connected the riddle to Don. I believe he is the reincarnation of President John F. Kennedy. He's African American, was born in 1964, is a friend to George Clooney, he was in the cast of the *Ocean's* movies, and he impersonated Sammy Davis, Jr. Now that I believed I had the answer, what was I supposed to do with it?

I decided to write out the whole riddle and solution, and send it to George Clooney. I felt this was maybe why Rosemary had said, "George needs you." Perhaps what he needed from me was the truth about reincarnation. So I wrote it all out, telling him all that had happened and who had appeared. I told him I did not want anything from him, and that it was his business what he chose to do with the information. I told him that I felt the information was important to pass on, as all of these people had appeared in such a complex production.

The only direct mailing address I could find for George was to his Production Company, *Smoke House Pictures*. I had already contacted Don Bauer, who, like George, was a producer with a production company, and had reached him successfully through his production company. Then I realized the whole riddle and the cast had produced a wonderful production. From all this, I decided the best way to reach George would be to send it to him via his production company.

I sent the letter by registered mail on September 4th, 2008, and I know from tracking it through the post office that it arrived at *Smoke House Pictures* on September 11th. I believe its arrival on this date was again Divine Timing! The timing and detail that went into this riddle were amazing. I am honoured that they appeared to me. I was so happy to have finally solved this riddle and to pass on what I'd discovered. I have no idea what George did with the information.

The only piece I was missing to the solution when I sent it to George was the connection to Marilyn and Carl Sandburg. The fact that Carl had written about Abraham Lincoln was another clue to confirm that the goal was to have me think of Lincoln when looking at Sammy sitting in the armchair. I did not discover this connection until years later, which for me really helped tie the entire solution altogether.

Even though I had no intention of releasing this information to the public at the time, I now believe it is important for people to know that we do come back in different roles, lifetime after lifetime. I felt this riddle was so significant that I had to include it in our story, as this is how Elvis was able to prove to me that we'd had other lifetimes together.

8

THE BLUE-NOSE HEALER
AND THE MYTHIC CALL

After the Alaskan cruise and solving the riddle, I felt guided to continue moving forward, reading and learning as much as I could about my spiritual gifts. People started showing up who needed my help. Since the week of September 11th, 2008, I'd had the opportunity to share healing energy with some women I knew. One of them was having health issues, and I had told her about my Elvis connection and the fact that I turned blue. She came to see me, and while we were talking, my hands began to vibrate. She then told me my nose had turned blue. I then put my hands on her shoulders until my nose went back to normal colour. This was the first time I had turned blue since the April Angelic Healing workshop, and I realized that if this was one of my gifts, I wanted to be open to using it to help those around me. I prayed that I would be sent those I could help the most.

The next week, everyone that I met seemed to be upset or hurting in some way. When I talked to them and they told me their problems, my nose would turn blue. So again, I would place my hands on them until my nose went back to normal.

My Angelic Healing instructor told me I was able to do distance healing, so when I phoned my girlfriend and found out she was sick, I said, "Let's see if I can send you healing energy." We got off the phone and both sat down in meditation. After ten minutes she called back and said I should stop, because she needed to make supper. She said she really wanted to sleep because it felt like she had been given a full body massage.

Every day that week, my nose turned blue until I touched the person who needed healing. I had Friday off from work, so I met two women from my previous place of employment for lunch. One of them had been in a car accident that week, and was experiencing pain in her neck. At the end of our lunch I told them about Elvis, and then my hands started to vibrate. I also told them that whenever I'm supposed to touch someone my nose turns blue!

They looked at me and said, "Your nose is blue," so I put my hands on my friend who had been in the car accident. After a few minutes of feeling the energy flowing, she did not want me to take my hands away. Elvis now called me, "The Blue-nose Healer!"

THE ROSE OF SHARON

On November 11th, 2008 – Remembrance Day – I was guided by my spirit guides to research the Rose of Sharon on the internet. I was not sure why. I did find that some people refer to Jesus as the Rose of Sharon, and it is also the name of some beautiful flowering plants.

As I continued my search, I was guided to the website of the Sacred Rose Council, and on that site was a link to a video created in 2007. I was intrigued by the title, *The Mythic Call* and decided to watch it. I became more and more shocked as I watched, as the video seemed to be about my life, the experiences from my past, and maybe about my future.

The video said it was A Love Story. It mentioned Blue Star Medicine, and the word Rem "ember." It mentioned the "Flame of Magdalene Awakens the Roses." It was about a wedding between Christ Osiris Dawn Star, and Mary Isis Sophia Magdalene. It mentioned the Hopi Elders, and the date December 21st, 2012. Was this video really about my life? I did not know what to think about this latest information, and if these were possibly other past lives of mine!

There was so much in the video that reminded me of my life that I compared the video with experiences in my life and discovered the following similarities:

- At the beginning of the video it states, "It's a love story." Elvis told me that our story is "A Love Story."

- The video mentions the return of the Blue Star Embers and Rem "ember." I had started to write my book and Abraham gave me the title, "Remember."

- It talked about a woman who will bring Blue Star Medicine and the power being in your hands. My nose turns blue and my hands vibrate when I am to give healing energy to someone.

- It also mentions the Beginning, the Tree of Life and the Garden. I have also regressed into the lifetime of Eve and have always felt I was her.

- A wedding is mentioned. Elvis says I am his Twin Flame and that we were once one being, but were split apart.

On April 11th, 2008, I had a dream about a pillow with wedding bands on it and I felt I was to pick one. I heard the words "The Bridegroom cometh." I also heard Elvis singing "Lay Your Head Upon My Pillow" and "It's Impossible."

- The video made reference to a New Jerusalem and shows the Star of David. I had purchased the triangular tanzanite ring & pendant, which reminded me of the Star of David. Elvis's grandmother on his mother's side was Jewish and his great-great-great-grandmother was full-blooded Cherokee (Morning Dove White).

I wondered what all of this information meant and if I would get more clarification. There just seemed to be too many similarities for it to be coincidence!

Throughout it all, I continued to meditate and connect with Elvis.

9
A ROMANTIC MESSAGE

On Saturday May 9th, 2009, without warning, Elvis went missing from my meditation. My last communication from him was that morning, and then that was it. Elvis had been appearing in my meditations and connecting to me inwardly at least twice a day for almost two-and-a-half years. Friends kept saying he was supposed to come back in 2009, and he told me himself he was coming.

Then, one more thing happened. On Sunday May 10th, I enjoyed watching the video *He Touched Me* (a Gaither Production) which is about Elvis and the gospel groups he loved to sing with. The last part of the DVD is about his funeral, which I did not watch. When it was finished I shut off the DVD player and set the remote down on my coffee table. The television was still on and set to AV1. Suddenly, of its own accord, the blue power light on the DVD player came back on, and the video began to play again. The first full length song Elvis sang was *I'll Remember You*. After listening to that song again, I shut off both the DVD player, and the television, realizing that Elvis had wanted to re-connect to me in this way.

This song was one of my favorite Elvis songs, and our love story was all about remembering! The words, "To your arms someday I'll return to stay" was a promise I felt he would somehow keep.

This song was written by a Hawaiian, Kui Lee, who died in 1966 from lymph gland cancer. On January 14th, 1973, Elvis performed the *Aloha from Hawaii* concert and raised $75,000 for the Kui Lee Cancer Fund.

On May 12th, 2009, I had a business meeting in a small town south of the city. When I arrived, I parked in a public parking lot. In front of my car was a park bench with the back boards missing. The bench was positioned sideways. For some reason, I noticed that the cement base was painted a light grey. This was an odd place for a broken bench, I thought.

During my meditation that night, I was shown Elvis sitting on a bench at a bus stop. He was dressed in a light grey-blue suit with a black shirt. He appeared as a younger Elvis, with both his hair and sideburns cut short. The bench was turned sideways so I only saw his profile. My spirit guides told me he was waiting. I was not sure what he was waiting for, and I wondered if perhaps he had been sitting on the bench in the parking lot in front of my car?

Two days later, during my meditation, I felt pain in the palms of both my hands (like a stigmata). Then I began to feel vibrations, and an image appeared of Jesus hanging on the cross. This upset me, and I wondered if I would actually experience a stigmata. Why had Jesus appeared to me hanging on the cross? Why had He returned to my meditation now, and why had Elvis gone missing? Before Elvis' first appearance to me, Jesus had appeared regularly, and now Jesus was appearing again. I had so many questions.

On Friday May 22nd, I received a message from Archangel Gabriel, who said, "Elvis has left the building. Everything is moving ahead as it is destined to be. You will meet him again very soon." I was surprised by how Gabriel talked about Elvis leaving the building, plus I was not sure how I would meet him again, especially since he was on the other side. I just needed to trust that I was being guided. My life was certainly not dull!

That weekend I took another Angelic Healing workshop, with a different instructor, to learn about working with Mother Mary, Gaia (Mother Earth) and the Archangels. On the Sunday of the workshop, the last thing we did was work in twos. We took turns working with an Archangel, and asking for a message for the other person. The woman I was working with said she would work with Archangel Michael, who is associated mostly with the colour blue.

Part of the message she received for me from Michael was about me finding an office or room outside my home to do healings. He said he would protect me, and there would always be Angels guarding my door. He told me I would be busy, and that an office was being prepared for me. Then the message changed, and it seemed like Elvis was speaking to me.

"You are balanced and 'in tune,'" he said. "Do not be Blue my love. I am not far. I am waiting for you with this next journey. You know Blue Hawaii ~ it is ours. All our Love, Blessing and Peace."

The woman who received this message for me knew nothing about my connection to Elvis, and understandably asked, "What is this about?" She seemed very confused by the last part of the message.

So I explained about my connection to Elvis, and that he'd been missing from my meditations since May 9th. We'd been together constantly since June of 2006, and I'd been feeling quite upset about this separation. What did Elvis mean by his message?

I researched the movie *Blue Hawaii* on the internet and discovered that it was Elvis' eighth movie. It was released in the United States on November 22, 1961 (11/22/1961). I added the numbers of the year together (1 + 9 + 6 + 1 = 17 and 1 + 7 = 8) and found they equaled an eight. I realized that the release date was my number – eleven twenty-two plus Elvis' number eight (11/22/8) and it was his eighth movie!

I then began to receive more messages from Archangel Gabriel, encouraging me to stay focused on Love, Peace, and Wisdom. In the mornings, when I first woke up, I began to hear more love songs on the radio. Gabriel said Elvis wanted me to know these love songs were meant for me. Gabriel himself explained that Elvis was expressing his love for me through these songs. Sometimes I would feel my lip quiver, and I would be told that Elvis was sending me a kiss. This was all so amazing!

On June 2nd, Elvis told me he was still around me. He had not left me totally, and said I should trust in Divine Timing. The next day he told me that all was happening as it should. He told me he loved me so much, and that I should not be sad that he was not communicating with me all the time. He told me there were things he must do on that side to help us complete this next journey together. He also told me I was so beautiful!

On June 4th, Elvis let me know he would not be communicating with me much longer. He told me how much he loved and treasured me. He told me there were many spirit beings around me, protecting me while we were apart. He also said this was only a temporary separation. He told me to keep my thoughts on Love, Peace, and Wisdom, just as Archangel Gabriel had advised.

June 5th, 2009, was the third anniversary of Elvis' first appearance in my meditation and, again, it was the Elvis Anniversary Celebration in Tupelo. If he had not left us so suddenly, Elvis would now have been seventy-four years of age. As I sat meditating, Elvis appeared in his black leathers carrying a suitcase in his right hand. He told me I should let him go, and that he would find me. He then turned, and with his back to me, Elvis walked out of my meditation from where he'd first walked in, three years before to the day!

Then on June 11th, Jesus appeared in my meditation. He said he had always been with me. He said he understood that I was looking for Elvis, but told me that Elvis was on his way.

10
HAY HOUSE CRUISE

I had planned another Alaskan cruise for July of 2009, this time with Hay House. I was not sure if Elvis was waiting for this journey to reappear in my meditation. But I was hopeful this is what he had meant by his message.

On the morning of July 10th I was at the airport early, my seat selected back in January. I noticed a young man pacing at the boarding gate, and then, just before we began to board, the flight attendant called my name. She asked me if I would mind moving across the aisle from my assigned seat, so this young man could sit with his wife. Of course, I said yes. Once aboard, the young couple kept thanking me. It turned out they were on their honeymoon. I would have been sitting between them, with one of them sitting across the aisle from me. Even though the aircraft seemed full, in my new seat, no one sat next to me. That seat remained vacant. I had the feeling this seat was for Elvis.

This was my first trip to Seattle, and I was eager to get to the hotel. While I was checking in, they upgraded my room to a suite on the eleventh floor. I was now in room 1121 with my door facing room 1122. I felt Elvis had arranged for me to stay in this beautiful two-room suite. That afternoon, I took a city tour with Gray Line Tours. I was told if there were not many people it would be a small white van, but if it was a larger group it would be a large *blue* bus. When it arrived, it was a large blue bus! The bus was full – except for the empty seat beside me.

During our tour, the driver pointed out the sites and views of the city. I was startled when he suddenly began talking about Elvis, who had been there in 1963 while filming *It Happened at the World's Fair*. I had forgotten about that movie, and the fact that he had spent time in Seattle.

When I got back to my room, I felt Elvis' presence. He said in the note from May that he was waiting for me with this next journey, and he was there with me! When Elvis makes his presence known to me, I feel his loving energy around me and in me, from the top of my head. It feels like a wonderful wave of loving energy flowing through me.

Our ship departed from Seattle on July 11th and, at the pier, I met some of the female passengers I've since kept in touch with. Although I had a cabin to myself, I could feel Elvis' loving presence, and knew he was there with me.

BLUE DIAMONDS

We stopped at some of the same ports as my previous 2008 Alaskan cruise, the first being Juneau where I had purchased the blue diamond and tanzanite jewelry. When we arrived in Juneau this time, I felt Elvis encouraging me to buy a bigger blue diamond. Again, this is not something I would normally do, as I am not an extravagant person.

I had a VIP card for Venetian Jewelers from the shopping guide onboard. They were offering a free pendant for just trying on one of the rings, so I thought I would just go and have a look at the rings and pendants. I really thought that was my intention! I was told to ask for the Store Manager to get the best price on jewelry. I told some of the women I was going to look at the rings and get the free pendant, or, perhaps, I might buy one.

I'm not sure exactly what happened. When I asked for the Manager, she introduced me to the Assistant Manager. I told him I wanted to try on rings with a blue diamond, and get that free pendant. So he showed me a ring that had small blue diamonds on the side and a single white diamond at the top. He then offered me a 1.0 carat white diamond ring to try on with blue diamonds on the side, but it was too large. When I told him it should be a single blue diamond on the top, he showed me a blue diamond with white diamonds on the side. That's when I heard Elvis saying, "No, it should have a single blue diamond on the top, and blue diamonds on the side." When I relayed these specifications to the man he said it would be no problem to change the single white diamond to a single blue diamond in the ring that already had the blue diamonds on the side. The single blue diamond turned out to be .71 carats, which seemed to me to be an odd size for a diamond.

So I ended up designing the ring the way I wanted it – or the way Elvis wanted it! I had never done anything like this in my life, but Elvis had always bought jewelry for himself and his friends, so he knew what he liked. I also noticed a pendant I liked that matched the ring, with alternating blue and white diamonds. Before I even knew what had happened, I had purchased both the ring and the pendant, and both at a very good price They told me the ring would be ready in a couple of hours, so I could come back and pick it up. I left the store in a daze, not knowing exactly what had just happened, but loving my purchases!

After I picked up my jewelry and returned to the ship, one of the women said, "Let me see your ring!" Apparently she'd gone into the store after I had already left, and when she told them I was coming to look at the rings, they said, "Oh do you mean Eve? She's already been here and bought a ring." So the women back on board were all excited, and wanted to know the story of my purchase.

For the formal evening, I felt I was to wear my long blue dress, and the photographer took two pictures in front of a green background. She had me stand for one, and then sit on a stool for the other. For the sitting shot, she had me pose with my head tilted to the right, with my right hand under my chin, palm down, just touching my neck below my chin. When I picked up the photo the next day, it was printed on a night sky background, so my head was surrounded with twinkling blue stars.

Posed as I was, with my hand under my chin, I was reminded of Da Vinci's painting of the Last Supper. In the *Da Vinci Code* movie, it was theorized that the person to the right of Jesus was Mary Magdalene. The painting shows one of the disciples with his hand placed under her chin in the same position as I had my hand. Was this perhaps a sign of a past life with Jesus?

The rest of the cruise was very enjoyable, and I knew Elvis was with me again. During my flight home from Seattle, I once again sat alone with an empty seat beside me, but, as before, I felt Elvis was right there with me. He connected to me a few more times after I got home, but not as often as before. I was again waking up in the morning to love songs playing on the radio. Elvis would often sing to me.

A RING FROM ELVIS

I had not paid much attention to the setting of the latest blue diamond ring, or how many diamonds it held until I got home. When I was describing it to a girlfriend over the phone, I really looked at it closely for the first time. The beautiful setting surrounds the blue diamond in the centre with many smaller diamonds. The centre blue diamond is .71 carats, which equals eight. When I counted the small diamonds surrounding it, there were exactly seventy-one, which equals another eight, not including the large diamond. As I began describing the ring in detail to my friend, I noticed the setting was in the shape of an eight, with the blue diamond at the top of the eight. The blue diamond is raised about half an inch above my finger, and the bottom point of the diamond creates a heart shape in the empty space above my finger. There are a total of eleven blue diamonds, including the large one.

When I also added up the total diamond carats, I found they equaled 2.06. Again, another eight (infinity and Elvis' number). I knew Elvis designed and had me purchase this ring, which was the most beautiful piece of jewelry I'd ever seen, let alone owned. The setting was a modified version of the Venus ring design, and it fit best on my left ring finger. Was this intended to be my engagement ring?

One of my friends looked at the ring and said it looked like a man and a woman's ring together. Elvis was always telling me that we are One, so I felt this ring signified our being One. I began to think there might be more information about this ring I still did not know. I was curious about Priscilla's wedding ring, but I didn't think he would have had me purchase a ring like either her engagement or wedding ring. At the time, I was unable to find a good close up of her ring, for which I was actually very thankful.

I was able to find a good picture of Elvis' ring, and it did look similar to the wider portion of mine. On October 10th, he confirmed my findings. He said, "Eve, my love, it is no coincidence that the ring is similar. The diamonds may not be the same, but the eight and the rows have been made so you would notice the similarity. I love you."

That fall, I also felt guided to enroll in a Huna - Hawaiian Shamanism workshop. The same woman that taught my second Angelic Healing workshop had been to Hawaii to learn Huna personally from a Hawaiian Shaman. I felt I should learn these traditional Hawaiian healing methods and felt it was an honour to have this opportunity.

11
ELVIS IN PERSON

After the cruise Elvis, did not communicate with me as often as he had been, but he told me we are connected on all levels. Sometimes I would wake up to him singing me a love song, such as *Unchained Melody*. Other times, he would give me more profound messages such as, "I am not coming to SAVE the world the way the church has been telling the people. And I am not coming to take the dead out of the ground. I am coming because of LOVE, LOVE FOR YOU and LOVE FOR THE WORLD." I wondered if he was coming back, or if he was already back? If he said we are connected on all levels, what exactly did that mean?

On the Hay House cruise, I had enjoyed meeting many writers in the group, and found I wanted to re-connect with them. With that in mind, I decided to attend the Celebrate Your Life Conference being held in Scottsdale, Arizona, in November 2009. I wanted to learn more about spiritual topics, and to meet more like-minded people. The event was being held at the J.W. Marriott Desert Ridge in Scottsdale from November 13th - 16th. I booked my flight for November 11th with the intention of visiting Sedona on the 11th or 12th, if I could make the arrangements.

Before I left home I was told I would meet Elvis in person at the Conference. I was told I would know Elvis by his eyes, and that he would find me. I had no idea what to expect, or what might happen. He had stopped communicating to me again. The messages I was receiving were now from Archangels Michael and Gabriel. This was truly a lesson in faith, and in trusting that what I was being told was the truth.

I left Calgary on November 11th, 2009 (11/11/11). I booked the trip through my travel agent, and she booked me on Flight 173, which equaled eleven, leaving at 6:50 a.m. – another eleven – and sitting in seat 11C. We left from Gate 22. When we landed in Phoenix, we taxied up to Gate 11B. I noticed the numbers eleven and twenty-two were everywhere.

I took a shuttle to the hotel and checked in. Having been up since 1:30 a.m., I was very tired after the flight. After a quick nap, I went to the front desk and managed to book a Sedona tour for the next day, Thursday the 12th. For dinner, I went to the Blue Sage restaurant. Everything on the menu was listed with the word blue (e.g. blue corn, veggie burger with blue cheese, etc.). I was not surprised, since I'd been told that Elvis was going to appear! I then retired to my room for the evening.

The next morning I boarded the tour van to Sedona just after 7:30 a.m. On our way north out of Phoenix, we toured the countryside and stopped to shop in Jerome. We arrived in Sedona in time for a group lunch, and then spent the afternoon on our own exploring and shopping. I just loved Sedona, and wandered around the main streets enjoying the shops. As I passed one shop, there were two store clerks standing outside talking. Just as I approached, one fellow sneezed, and the other fellow said, "Bless you!" The fellow that sneezed had dark hair and sideburns, and said, "Thank you, thank you very much!" and smiled a big smile at me!

Before we left Sedona some of the passengers talked our driver into stopping at the Bell Vortex for a quick visit, so we got out and walked around. By the time we got back to our hotel it was about 7:00 p.m. There was still no sign of Elvis and I was getting discouraged. When I sat down in mediation, I got another message from the Archangels saying he would find me, and not to worry.

The event began the next morning with a full day workshop delivered by James Van Praagh. I sat next to a woman and her daughter. At noon they served a lunch buffet out on the lawn, and I planned to sit with these ladies. By then I had stopped thinking about Elvis.

Placing my jacket on a chair, I headed over to the buffet and got in line. While I was putting salad and tomatoes on my plate I dropped a tomato on the sidewalk, and said, "Oh no!" The man in front of me turned around to see what the problem was. He looked at me with the bluest eyes, and then down at the tomato, and said, with a very gracious English accent, "Kick it under the table!"

"I can't do that" I said in dismay, to which he replied, "Yes you can, kick it under the table," and then he laughed at me as I did. When we got to the end of the line his lady friend appeared, and he asked, "May we join you?"

"Of course," I said, and told him where they could find my jacket on the chair. Introductions were then made all around, and Justin and Trudy joined us for lunch.

Sitting opposite me at the big round table, Justin asked me what I did. I told him I was a Healer to Healers, and that my business was called, "Blue Star Medicine." At his request, we exchanged business cards. Once lunch was over we returned to the workshop for the afternoon session. We talked some more after the workshop, and then we kept running into each other between workshops. Later he told me he'd had a past life regression with a woman in Sedona called Sakina Blue Star, on November 12th – the same day I was there. When they saw my business name was Blue Star Medicine, they knew we were supposed to meet.

I told them of my connection to Elvis and the fact that I knew he had been Jesus. I also told them he told me he would meet me at the Conference, and that I would know him by his eyes. Here was Justin with the bluest eyes, and he kind of looked like Jesus.

At that point, amazingly, Justin told me that his past life memory was that he had been Jesus. Now when I meditate and Jesus shows up, he looks like Justin. The three of us spent quite a bit of time together. I could not stop staring at his eyes!

I was booked to also hear Dr. Brian Weiss speak. During his session he did two past life regressions with the whole audience. My first regression took me to a wedding. I was Mary. It was my wedding day, and I was marrying Jesus at Cana. I saw his face, and I knew it was Elvis.

During the second regression, Dr. Weiss instructed us to "go to an experience of being in your Mother's womb, and see yourself being born." When I did this, I thought I would go to my current lifetime, but instead I went to the lifetime of Elvis and Jesse. Watching from above, I saw my birth/death as Jesse, and Elvis' birth. This was a very emotional experience for me.

After these two regressions I needed to think about what I had just experienced. I had read Julia Ingram's book, *The Lost Sisterhood - The Return of Mary Magdalene, the Mother Mary, and Other Holy Women*. I remembered reading that multiple women had memories of the same lifetimes, one of which was Mary Magdalene. Now I was having memories of my life with Jesus at our wedding! I knew my name had been Mary, but I was not sure about the name Magdalene. I felt very strongly that being married to Jesus was my truth.

As a result of my many years of reading and meditation, I have come to understand that the "over-Soul" is so large that it can split into smaller portions so it can return at the same or overlapping times. This creates parallel lifetimes, and allows the Soul to advance faster by having different experiences. These parallel lifetime experiences can depend on what the Soul needs to learn, or what karma needs to be cleared from previous lifetimes. I did wonder how many of the other Marys remembered being married to Jesus at Cana.

The next day I went with my new friends to hear Neale Donald Walsch. During his presentation he told us to ask God a question, sit quietly and listen, and then to write down the answer we received. So I asked God, where is EP? Is he here with me in someone else? Here is the answer I received: "Eve, he is there with you in Justin, and in spirit of Christ. You know him by his eyes, just as you were told he would be with you. He found you just as we said he would. I know you were expecting him to be with you, but this is not the way it is meant to be at this time. He is a portion of the Christ. All is as it should be. Bless you, Mother/Father GOD."

Never underestimate the Divine! I realized that Justin was a parallel life of Elvis, and a portion of Jesus. He was thirty-five years old, which was an eight. I also remembered the "piece of eight" pendant, and the significance of that coin now started to make more sense. Was Justin equal to one real, or one eighth of a "piece of eight"? I did not know if there were eight individuals currently on the planet that were portions of Jesus, but I knew I had met two of them.

I was amazed and disappointed to put it mildly, that my love was not there in the flesh, even though he was, but not the way I had hoped. This was such a shock. Then I wondered, was his Trudy also a part of me? I realized I didn't really want to know the answer to this question. Life seemed to be getting more and more complicated and confusing!

I was happy to meet these two, and felt very comfortable talking with them about my life experiences with Elvis. I told them I was hoping to write a book about my life. When they told me they listen to Elvis' music all the time, I suggested they order Larry Geller's book about Elvis, as it would help him understand his life. Justin and Trudy were staying at a different hotel, so when the conference ended that afternoon, it was time to say goodbye.

I flew home the next day on November 17th, which was an eight. My trip home was on Flight 245, which equaled eleven, leaving at 11:18 a.m. another eleven, and I was sitting in seat 8D. I knew Elvis was there, and could feel him sitting with me on that flight.

When I got home I checked my emails and found a newsletter from The Sacred Rose Council, which arrived on 11/11/2009:

> *"11:11:11 ~ The Opening of the Rose Stargate 33 ~*
>
> *This year 2009 is an 11 year and thus this eleventh month of November blesses us with an 11:11 vibration for the whole month.*
>
> *When we look at the clock at 11:11 it makes us pause and perhaps reminds us of Oneness and of the powerful gateway that this is!*
>
> *November 11th and 29th are both incredibly powerful days numerologically, as they*

hold the 11:11:11 vibration of 33, which is a Master Teacher Vibration holding the energies of the Divine Christ Consciousness. 11 is a gateway number, and carries the vibrations of heightened intuition, vision, revelation, illumination, high ideals and equal balance of masculine and feminine. It also carries the vibration of the transformation of the physical into the Divine. The two pillars of 11 represent a gateway and initiation into the Light!!! It means walking through a portal and letting go and releasing the past and everything that is not serving your highest good or the highest good of the planet, so you can walk through the portal to embrace and live in the Light.

So this month, let us bring our awareness to this mystical and visionary vibration... On November 11th and 29th, 11-11-11 let us join together in sacred ceremony and global meditation wherever we are, at 11:11 a.m. and/or p.m. or any time during these days to attune to the Christ Consciousness Master Teacher Vibrations!!

With Divine Love and Deep Blessings of the 11:11:11 Vibration, Deborah El'elia Jahmika Christos aka: Deborah Knighton Tallarico"

For me, this message was a very powerful ending to my trip to meet Elvis (Jesus) in person, especially since he appears in my meditation as he looked at age thirty-three and the age at which Jesus died. My flight left from Gate 22 and we arrived in Phoenix at Gate 11B, which totaled thirty-three. Plus, my flight number, time of departure, and my seat number were all elevens, which was another thirty-three. This all happened on 11/11/11, which was the opening of Rose Stargate 33. Had I gone through a portal and met Elvis (Jesus) on the other side? I knew that this trip had far more meaning than I understood!

12

HAWAIIAN CRUISE
AND A PROPOSAL

I often watch *The Gaither's Gospel Hour* on Friday night television, and noticed their next cruise in August of 2010 was to Hawaii. I felt it was important to go on this cruise with Bill and Gloria Gaither, and many of the Gospel singers from their television program. I also thought taking a cruise was a good way to see more than one Hawaiian island. When I asked my friend Sheila if she wanted to go with me, it wasn't long before she said yes. Sheila also liked Gospel music. We were both very excited!

We started planning our trip in November 2009, even though our cruise was not for another nine months. When we discussed going all that way just for the cruise, we realized it would be a waste not to stay longer. Neither of us had been to Hawaii before, so we decided to go five days earlier and stay in Honolulu.

It was almost Christmas and I was curious about why Elvis wanted me to go to Hawaii. He loved Hawaii, and he loved Gospel music, especially the Gaither's music. He kept reassuring me it was the right thing for me to do.

Planning and anticipating this trip was starting to get the best of me, so I asked Elvis if we were getting married in Hawaii. I knew one of the island stops on the cruise was Kauai, where Elvis had filmed the wedding scene in the movie, *Blue Hawaii.* "Yes," he replied, we would get married in Hawaii. He said, "This is our destiny!"

On December 10th, I asked him if we would be married on Kauai. His response was, "Yes, you are right, we will be married on Kauai in August of next year. TRUST that this was planned a long time ago. I love you so much. Bless you my lovely wife."

His message on December 12th was, "The trip to Hawaii is in August because that is the eighth month. This is on purpose, as I had planned to go back to Hawaii after my tour, but you know that. Don't you think it is fitting that we marry on Kauai?"

"Will you marry me? I shouldn't just plan and expect you to go without asking. I was going to wait to ask you, but you already know. This is proper. I don't want any misunderstandings between us. I know we can know each other's thoughts, but communication is paramount. I love you so much, and want it to be known by the world that "Love Never Dies." You are too precious to me. Death could not keep us apart. I am here and have been with you for many years. Yes, it wasn't until college that I started to make my presence known to you. It's been a long time, Baby! Bless you and all my love!"

Of course I said, "YES!"

On December 13th, I wondered if I should buy a wedding ring. Hearing my thoughts he said, "A ring is a good idea, but not necessary. We will get the ring in Hawaii. We will buy it together. I love you!"

13
ANGEL CARD READING

In June 2010, I took Charles Virtue's Angel Certification Program (ACP) course. I was not sure why I was taking this course, and I didn't really know what it was about. I just felt I should attend. I thought Charles would be teaching another healing modality. During the class we learned to work with Angel Cards and did readings for each other. If I had known what Charles planned to teach I would not have registered for this class, as I was not really interested in giving readings. I was afraid I would not receive any information for the person to whom I was giving a reading.

I met some new people while attending the course. The first reading we did was without a card deck. I was very new to using cards, and the idea of trying to receive information for another person without cards was quite frightening. Without knowing the person, we were to listen to tune into the spirit guides to learn about the other person. Charles told us that once we received any messages, we were to share that information with the person. I learned I did not need any cards to tap into messages for another person if I just listened. I found this amazing!

We each received an Angel card deck and Charles explained that we should have each person we read for pull three cards for their reading. They would do the same for us. They would think of a question or have an intention for the reading. The first card represented the past, the second the present, and the third the future. Just like the setting of my first blue diamond ring!

Then, on the last day, Sunday, June 20th, 2010, this is what happened: we paired up with another person, and then asked the Angels for information about abundance for that person. I read for my partner first, and asked Elvis and Archangel Michael for information about abundance for her. She picked three cards, "Romance," "Retreat," and "Abundance." I felt very strongly that there was a man in her life, and told her there was lots of love and romance. I also sensed that the retreat was a romantic getaway with a commitment involved. I told her this commitment would bring an abundance of love into her life.

When I put my hand on the Romance card, Elvis said, "Eve, you know I'm all about Romance!" I sensed he was smiling! I told her about my connection on the other side, and said he was all about Romance. Then I told her it was Elvis. She reached over the cards and grabbed my hands and said, "You won't believe what happened to me on the way here today! I followed a car with the license plate, *Elvis 1!*" She told me that last year she was married on the Island of Kauai, and they had Elvis' song, *Can't Help Falling in Love with You* played at their wedding. They also drove to the Coco Palms Resort to see where Elvis had filmed, *Blue Hawaii*. I realized this was the commitment and romantic getaway that I had picked up in my reading.

When I told her Elvis was with us, we both started to cry. This was such a powerful and profound experience for us both. This must have been planned such a long time ago. I almost did not go to this course, and then I would have missed meeting her and having this connection. I believe there is a reason we met each other.

When I finished the reading she looked at me and said, "You know he is Jesus..."

I *had* known this, of course, but this was the first time someone else had confirmed it for me. No one had ever said this before. It was all so overwhelming!

14
WEDDING JITTERS

I decided to tell my friend Bridget that Elvis had proposed. Then on July 12th, Bridget received a notice that a package had arrived for her at the bus depot. It was her wedding dress from her first marriage that a friend in another city had been storing for her for many years. She knew it was coming, but had no idea when it would arrive. Had her husband lived, the day it arrived would have been their 31st wedding anniversary. I happened to see her that day, just after she had picked it up, so she showed it to me. I noticed right away that the style of her dress was very similar to the wedding dress that Joan Blackman wore in the role of Maile, in the movie, *Blue Hawaii*. Because she knew my story, Bridget asked me if I might like to borrow it for my trip. After thinking about it I declined her offer, as I felt this would have been just a bit too strange. I really did not know what Elvis had planned.

A few days later I went for lunch with another friend, and during lunch she said, "Eve, while you are in Honolulu, you should go to the house where Elvis sang the song *Can't Help*

Falling in Love with You from the movie, *Blue Hawaii.*" The very next day I heard that song no fewer than six times. I played it twice before I went to the hair salon, and then, while I was there, they played it four times on their CD player!

Some of the women at work must have picked up on something and began to speculate, saying things like, "I bet you and your friend Sheila will come back married!" Little did they know this would be true for me! There were very few people in my life that knew of my experiences and inner relationship with Elvis. All this talk of weddings was starting to make me increasingly nervous, but I was very happy I was going to Hawaii.

Although I was once again in constant communication with Elvis, he would not tell me what was going to happen when we got to Hawaii. He said it would be a surprise. The second week of our trip was the cruise with Bill and Gloria Gaither, which they were calling "The Hawaiian Homecoming Cruise." Elvis had truly loved to sing Gospel music, and had recorded the Gaither's song *He Touched Me.* Hawaii had always been like a second home to Elvis so, to me, it felt like he was going home.

15
BLUE HAWAII

I knew Elvis loved Hawaii, and with his message to me in May 2009, "You know Blue Hawaii ~ it is ours," I felt I needed to see it for myself. But while Sheila and I were good friends, I had not shared much with her about my experiences with Elvis. I was very cautious, as I did not want it to affect our friendship, or our trip. So I continued to keep it private. Elvis had told me he was all about romance, and to expect the unexpected while I was in Hawaii. I had no idea what was going to happen, but I knew that with Elvis, nothing was impossible.

Once Sheila and I were settled in our hotel on the evening of August 9th, we decided to get some dinner and then do some sightseeing. It was wonderfully warm, and the ocean breeze was heavenly. Tired from our long flight and time zone change, we decided to head back to our hotel for the evening after a brief walk around the shops.

The next day we explored Honolulu on foot, and then took the free shuttle to the Hilo Hattie store. While we were looking at clothes, a salesperson from the jewelry counter approached me, and asked me to pick a key to a treasure chest. I was not sure what this was about. Once I opened the chest, I selected a coupon for a discounted amount on a pearl. She told me to choose an oyster from a bowl, and I would be guaranteed at least one pearl. Once I picked an oyster, she handed me a knife and told me to tap the oyster three times. She rang a bell and I said, "Alo-ha." She opened the oyster.

There lay a single, perfect white pearl.

A WEDDING RING

I heard Elvis inwardly say it was for a ring, so I repeated that decision to the woman. When I told her it should be white gold, she showed me a setting with two small diamonds on each side, and two leaves that would encircle the pearl once it was mounted. Then she pulled out a card and placed it on the counter. It identified the setting as, "**The Maile Leaf.**"

In shock I blurted out, "You have to be kidding!"

"No," she said, looking quite surprised by my reaction. So, I told her that Elvis was there with us, and then I told her some of my story about Elvis and the movie *Blue Hawaii*. I also told her the bride's name in the movie had been Maile.

"Oh, I love Elvis!" she exclaimed with a big smile. Suddenly I remembered that Elvis had told me we would buy the ring together, and I realized it was happening right now.

The card explained that the Maile Leaf grows on Maui, Kauai and the big Island of Hawaii. The Maile Lei was originally worn only by Royalty, and only for special ceremonies. Today this Lei is worn by the bride and groom during their wedding ceremony, or it can be given to someone that has achieved something special. The meaning of the Maile Lei is ALOHA (love) and HO'OHANOHANO (honour).

TWIN PEARLS FOR TWIN FLAMES

After reading the card I knew this was the right setting for the pearl, and that this would be my wedding ring! With the setting decided upon, she told me to pick another oyster and complete the same ritual. As she opened the next oyster, inwardly I heard Elvis say, "Twins" and yes, sure enough, there lay two identical white pearls that matched the first one. I realized these two "twin" pearls represented the two of us, in as much as we had been born as twins, Elvis and Jesse, and also as Elvis had told me we are Twin Flames.

In this moment he told me inwardly the twin pearls were for a pendant. When I asked her if she might have a pendant setting with the same design, she managed to find one for the two pearls. I was then instructed to pick another oyster. Again the woman opened it and, again, it was another pair of identical white pearls, exactly the same as the last three. I heard Elvis say these were for earrings. Then I picked another oyster, and as she opened it, there lay another matching single white pearl. When I asked Elvis inwardly what this one was for, he said it was for her – so she would remember us.

"Elvis said this one is for you so you will remember us," I explained, as she removed it from the oyster, and of course she gracefully thanked me.

I had now picked four oysters containing six identical white pearls with Elvis' guidance. I then picked one last oyster, and found it contained a single black pearl. I kept it, but did not mount it in a jewelry setting. The sales clerks were all dumbfounded. To have one person select six identical white pearls, including two sets of twins, was something they had never seen happen before.

While I was doing this, Sheila had continued shopping for other items in the store, leaving me alone with my oysters and pearls. When she came over to see how I was doing, she was understandably surprised that I had already purchased such treasures; this was only our first morning in Honolulu.

When we got back to the hotel and had a better look at the pendant, I realized the design, with one pearl on top of the other, created an eight. The white gold Maile leaves wound around both pearls confirmed to me even more that Elvis wanted me to purchase this jewelry, and how much he loved me.

I also discovered that the people of Oahu love Elvis. Everywhere you go there are pictures, books, CDs and souvenirs of him. I had not realized that back in 1961, he gave a concert performance to raise money to help build the *USS Arizona Memorial*. Without his help that memorial might not have been built, and people have not forgotten. To my surprise, I was learning even more about this man who called me his Twin Flame.

Sheila and I visited the Polynesian Cultural Centre on Wednesday, enjoyed a dinner cruise on Thursday and took the Circle Island tour on Friday. It was a busy week, but in just a few days we were able to see quite a bit of Oahu.

On Saturday, August 14th we checked out of the hotel and headed for the cruise ship. The island itinerary was Maui for two days, Hilo for one day, Kona for one day, Kauai for two days, then back to Honolulu for one more night before heading home.

THE CITY OF REFUGE

We both enjoyed going on some shore excursions on most of the islands, either together or separately. When we stopped in Kona I took a tour of Historic Kona which went to the City of Refuge, a very spiritual location. After spending some time meditating in one of the huts, I felt very connected to this place. The energy was very powerful, and I did not want to leave.

When I walked down to the ocean, I was delighted to see a green Hawaiian sea turtle swimming near the shore. The turtle has always held special meaning to the Hawaiians. Their name for it is Honu, which means an omen of good luck and long life! I later learned the turtle also symbolizes "the navigator" that is able to find its way home time and time again. The female green Hawaiian turtle will swim hundreds of miles to return to her own birthing place to lay her eggs.

In Hawaiian mythology the Honu is many things, among them "a living bridge that brings two lovers together."

The Honu is also mentioned in the fourth chant of the Kumilopo, the sacred Hawaiian chant of creation. The last two lines read:

> "Born is the turtle living in the sea
> Guarded by the Maile seedlings living on land."

I got goose bumps when I later made these profound connections regarding this seemingly chance encounter with the sea turtle, and the purpose of my visit to Hawaii. In so many ways, it actually did feel like I'd found my way home.

As I continued to explore this special place I followed the map they had given us when we arrived. Each spot was numbered with a description of the location or item to explain how people lived back when it was inhabited.

I learned that The City of Refuge had been a safe haven or sanctuary for those that may have broken a sacred law. If the offender was successful in reaching this place, the kahuna (priest or shaman) would perform a purification ceremony so he might once again return home. If the offender was not successful in reaching the Refuge, he would be killed.

There was not enough time to see the whole site as it stretched over a very large area, and the tour bus was on a tight schedule. I found it to be a very peaceful and sacred place, and I felt truly sad when I had to leave.

When I got back to the pier Sheila was waiting so we walked around the shops and got ice cream cones because it was so hot. As soon as we left the air conditioned shop, the ice cream started to melt. I've never seen ice cream melt so fast, and we laughed at how quickly it began running down my arm. I found a trash barrel to stand over while I finished it as fast as possible. That was the last ice cream I ate outdoors!

When we got back to the ship we set sail for Kauai, our last port before heading back to Honolulu. I knew Elvis had filmed the wedding scene for the movie, *Blue Hawaii* on this island. We were booked to go to a Luau on Thursday August, 19th at the Kilohana Plantation (Luau Kalamaku). During the day I decided to go on the Wailua River Cruise and Fern Grotto tour by myself. Before leaving for this excursion, I heard Elvis tell me to wear the new pearl ring on the ring finger of my left hand. I chose this tour because I wanted to get as close as possible to where Elvis had been while filming *Blue Hawaii*. I was totally shocked when we drove past the Coco Palms Resort on our way to the river cruise, and then again on the way back. As we passed the Coco Palms the tour driver said, "Elvis is alive and well at the Coco Palms!" Little did he know that Elvis was actually there on the tour bus!

A WEDDING

After departing from the bus we boarded the riverboat that would take us to the Fern Grotto. The boat had an overhead canopy with open air sides so we could easily view and enjoy the scenery on our journey. Our hosts told us that when we arrived, they would sing *The Hawaiian Wedding Song* in Hawaiian. When I heard this I suddenly knew this was where we would be married. Elvis had sung this song in the traditional Hawaiian language in *Blue Hawaii*, and now it would be our wedding song. I found myself overwhelmed with emotion!

During the beautiful relaxing two mile river journey, our hosts entertained us with stories and songs of the Wailua River Valley. A young hula dancer also taught us her traditional Hawaiian dance. I enjoyed the entertainment and I did attempt the hula.

Kauai is known as the Garden Island, and I began to understand why as we passed the beautiful, lush vegetation along the river. This land was apparently the birthplace of the island's Ali'i, or royalty and, in the past, only royalty was allowed to go to the Grotto.

After arriving at the Fern Grotto landing, we climbed out of our boat and began following a short winding path that would take us to the Grotto itself. There were roosters crowing and chickens clucking everywhere along the way. The other tourists seemed very fascinated by these birds. Apparently, during Hurricane Iniki in 1992, many domestic chickens escaped, and because there are no predators on Kauai the birds have flourished.

The path we followed was lined with beautiful tropical ferns. Then, as we came around a curve, I caught my first glimpse of the Fern Grotto just ahead at the end of the path. It was a small lava cave opening with more ferns growing all around. The Grotto is now protected, so we stood behind a railing on an observation deck set back just a bit from the Grotto itself. At one time, people were allowed to go right into the Grotto to be married. It was a very peaceful and beautiful setting, enhanced by the many tropical flowers and native Hawaiian plants all around.

In 2006, the Grotto had experienced significant flooding, and rocks from the ceiling fell in. Ferns in the Grotto grow upside down, hanging from the ceiling, and most of them were washed away. Because of this, the State closed it for safety reasons for almost a year while they repaired the damage and made it safe for visitors again. The ferns have since grown back, and it is once again very lush!

As I stood there, the musicians and singers asked us to gather 'round closer, and I felt Elvis' presence so strongly beside me. It was a surreal experience to be standing there with others, some of whom were renewing their marriage vows, and others who were wanting to be married in the sacred Hawaiian tradition. As I listened to the words of this beautiful song and gazed into the Grotto, tears rolled down my cheeks. I didn't want others to see, as I certainly appeared to be standing there alone. But I could feel Elvis right there by my side.

I was wearing my Maile leaf wedding ring that Elvis had helped design, and the Bride in the movie *Blue Hawaii* was Maile. Elvis did not appear as I had hoped, but I now know in my heart that we were married in the ancient Hawaiian tradition.

Because this land was the birthplace of the island's Ali'i, or royalty, and the sacred capital of ancient Kauai, I felt Elvis had put me in a special place of honour. I knew Elvis loved Hawaii, and had planned on returning to Kailua Bay on Oahu in 1977. I wondered now, had we lived together in Hawaii at another time? It really felt like I had come home with him. I had trouble leaving this place as it seemed truly sacred to me. But soon it was time to go and, as I walked back along the path to board the river boat again, I felt both happiness, and sadness. I had no idea what else Elvis might have planned!

Back on the ship I decided not to share my Fern Grotto experience with Sheila as we prepared for the evening Luau. To me, it felt like this Luau would be our Wedding Celebration. There were many people from the cruise that would be attending, and the Gaithers had arranged tour buses to transport us to the ranch.

Upon our arrival, each guest was given traditional purple and white orchid lei. They were so beautiful! The table to which Sheila and I were assigned was in the Blue section, and the number was 413, which equaled an eight. It was right in front of the stage, and adjacent to the Gaither's table. I realized Elvis had arranged for me to be in a place of honour, just as the words on the card stated, *"The meaning of the Maile lei is ALOHA (love) and HO'OHANOHANO (honour)."*

Sheila was surprised that we had such great seats, but I knew Elvis had arranged all of these surprises for me. I was very happy, and yet sad that he could not be there with me physically.

After the Luau, we headed back to our ship to depart for Honolulu. As we sailed away from Kauai I stood alone on the deck and cried, as deep in my heart it felt like I was leaving our home.

After the cruise, Sheila and I stayed for one more night in Honolulu. That evening we attended the Society of Seven show, with seven male impressionists. It seemed as if Elvis was repeatedly bringing impressionists into my life! I was given a seat next to the stage, once again in a place of honour. This was the last night for this particular group of seven as two of the entertainers were leaving the show. Suddenly I became part of the act from my seat! As he impersonated Tony Orlando, one of the entertainers sang, *Tie a Yellow Ribbon Round an Old Oak Tree.* As he sang the words "will you still want me?" he reached out and took my hand. It felt to me like it was Elvis asking the question. Predictably they also impersonated Elvis, and also asked for audience members to try and impersonate the King.

Then, one of the entertainers came over and asked me to smack his butt, and would not leave until I relented. Once I did, he told me he had just been kidding, but one of the other fellows felt left out so he also wanted me to smack his butt. By then the audience was howling with laughter. I knew Elvis loved to play jokes on friends and to make people laugh, and I felt pretty strongly that he was responsible for all this. The fellows then gave us high fives and shook our hands. It was a truly wonderful way to spend our last night in this paradise.

The next day was August 22nd, and by the time we ate and packed to leave the hotel it was time to head for the airport to get our 5:00 p.m. flight. Seven hours later we arrived in Calgary, and while Sheila was waiting for her sister to pick her up, my plan was to take a cab home. When I walked through the doors there were two limousine drivers standing just outside, so I decided to take a limo. When the driver gave me his business card it read EDDIE ROYAL, with a crown printed at an angle on the second D of Eddie – like a King. I knew Elvis had arranged this driver for me as well.

I realized that Elvis had lovingly arranged all of these romantic and wonderful events, and I will always cherish the memories of this trip. He is truly a romantic!

On September 19th, my one month anniversary of being married to Elvis, I was talking to my friend Lisa on the phone when I had a sudden feeling that someone was about to ring my doorbell with a delivery. At that same moment Lisa began telling me about a friend receiving a dozen blue roses from her boyfriend. Then she said that in the time she has known this woman, her boyfriend has sent her a dozen blue roses – twice! When I heard this, I realized that Elvis was visually sending me two dozen blue roses for our one month anniversary. He knows that my favourite flower is a blue rose!

When you connect to the eternal love of your Twin Flame, even from the other side, you come to understand the truth behind the phrase, "Love Never Dies!" My Twin Flame found me after his passing, and ever since that day he has continued to shower me with his love and blessings!

Our Love Story continues...

WORKS CITED

Bauer, Don. *All Shook Up*; White Hair Pictures, 1999.

Benson, Sally. *Viva Las Vegas*; Metro-Golden-Mayer (MGM), 1964.

Binder, Steve & Howe, Bones. *Elvis (The '68 Comeback Special)*; NBC TV Special, 1968.

Blackwell, Otis & Presley, Elvis. *All Shook Up*; Elvis Presley Music, 1956.

Bono, Sonny. *Baby Don't Go*; Reprise Records, 1964.

Brown, Dan. *The DaVinci Code*; Doubleday, 2003.

Brown, Harry & Lederer, Charles. *Ocean's Eleven*; Dorchester, Warner Bros. Pictures, 1960.

da Vinci, Leonardo. *The Last Supper*; 1495-1498.

Dickens, Charles. *A Christmas Carol*; Elliot Stock, 1890.

Dozier, William. *Batman TV Series*; American Broadcasting Company (ABC), 1966 – 1968.

Dyer, Wayne. *Getting in the Gap: Making Conscious Contact*; Hay House Inc., 2003.

Gaither, Bill and Gloria. *He Touched Me*; 1961 & (video) 2005.

Geller, Larry. *Leaves of Elvis' Garden - The Song of His Soul*; Bell Rock Publishing, 2007.

http://www.elvispresleybiography.net/

Honu-Green Hawaiian Sea Turtle

http://www.hawaiianlife.com/content/ hawaiian-honu-and-its-meaning

Ingram, Julia. *The Lost Sisterhood – The Return of Mary Magdalene, the Mother Mary, and Other Holy Women*; DreamSpeaker Creations, Inc. 2004.

Jahmika Christos, Deborah El'elia aka: Knighton Tallarico, Deborah. *11:11:11 ~ The Opening of the Rose Stargate 33 ~ 2009*; www.templeoftheheart.com

Kane, Bob & Goldsman, Akiva. *Batman & Robin*; Warner bros. Pictures, 1997.

Kristofferson, Kris. *For The Good Times*; 1970.

Lawrence, Anthony & Weiss, Allan. *Roustabout*; Hal Wallis Productions, 1964.

Lee, Kui. *I'll Remember You*; 1964.

Levine, Irwin & Brown, L. Russell. *Tie a Yellow Ribbon Round an Old Oak Tree*; 1973.

Lord, Walter. *A Night to Remember*; United Kingdom, 1958.

Mankiewicz, Joseph L. *All About Eve*; Twentieth Century Fox Film Corporation, 1950.

North, Alex and Zaret, Hy. *Unchained Melody*; 1955.

Pasetta, Marty. *Aloha from Hawaii*, Elvis Presley, 1973.

Peretti, Creatore, and Weiss. *Can't Help Falling in Love with You*; 1961.

Richmond, Ted. *It Happened at the World's Fair*; 1963.

Salem, Karlo. *The Rat Pack*; Home Box Office (HBO), 1998.

Schwartz, David R. *Robin and the 7 Hoods*; P-C Productions, 1964.

Sinclair (Red Song), Kevin & Gayford (White Star), Guy. *The Mythic Call*; The Sacred Rose Council, 2007. http://www.youtube.com/watch?v=NJrF-_duOoI

Sullivan, Ed. *Ed Sullivan Show*; CBS, 1964.

Wayne, Sid & Manzanero, Armando. *It's Impossible*. 1970.

Weiss, Allan & Kanter, Hal. *Blue Hawaii*; Hal Wallis Production. 1961.

Wells, George. *Where the Boys Are*; Euterpe, Metro-Golden-Mayer (MGM). 1960.

CPSIA information can be obtained at www.ICGtesting.com
Printed in the USA
BVOW05s2026070814

361874BV00002B/304/P